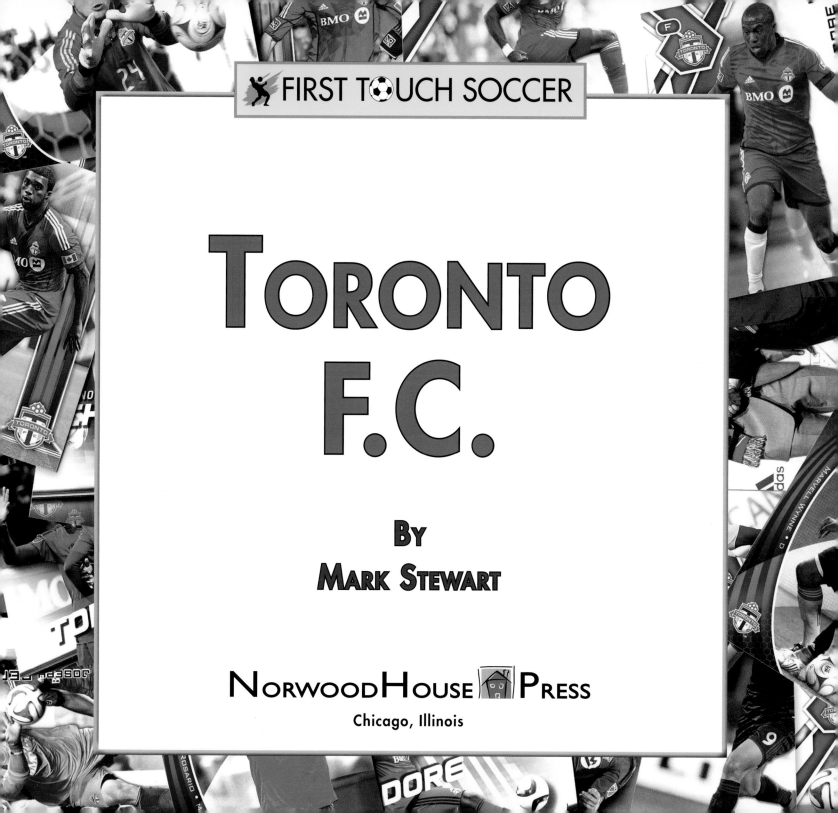

FIRST TOUCH SOCCER

TORONTO F.C.

BY
MARK STEWART

NORWOODHOUSE PRESS

Chicago, Illinois

NORWOODHOUSE🏠PRESS

P.O. Box 316598 • Chicago, Illinois 60631
For more information about Norwood House Press please visit our website at
www.norwoodhousepress.com or call 866-565-2900.

Photography and Collectibles:
The trading cards and other memorabilia assembled in the background for this book's cover and interior pages
are all part of the author's collection and are reproduced for educational and artistic purposes.

All photos courtesy of Associated Press except the following individual photos and artifacts (page numbers):
The Upper Deck Company LLC (6, 10 top, 16), Panini SpA (11 middle),
Topps, Inc. (10 bottom, 11 top & bottom, 22).

Cover image: David Kirouac/Associated Press

Designer: Ron Jaffe
Series Editor: Mike Kennedy
Content Consultants: Michael Jacobsen and Jonathan Wentworth-Ping
Project Management: Black Book Partners, LLC
Editorial Production: Lisa Walsh

LIBRARY OF CONGRESS CATALOGING-IN-PUBLICATION DATA
Names: Stewart, Mark, 1960 July 7- author.
Title: Toronto F.C. / by Mark Stewart.
Other titles: Toronto Football Club
Description: Chicago Illinois : Norwood House Press, 2017. | Series: First
   Touch Soccer | Includes bibliographical references and index. | Audience:
   Age 5-8. | Audience: K to Grade 3. | Description based on print version
   record and CIP data provided by publisher; resource not viewed.
Identifiers: LCCN 2016058984 (print) | LCCN 2017015630 (ebook) | ISBN
   9781684040896 (eBook) | ISBN 9781599538709 (library edition : alk. paper)
Subjects: LCSH: Toronto FC--Juvenile literature.
Classification: LCC GV943.6.T594 (ebook) | LCC GV943.6.T594 S84 2017 (print)
   | DDC 796.334/6309713541--dc23
LC record available at https://lccn.loc.gov/2016058984

This publication is intended for educational purposes and is not affiliated with any team, league, or association
including: Toronto Football Club, Major League Soccer, CONCACAF, or the Federation Internationale de Football
Association (FIFA).

302N--072017
Manufactured in the United States of America in North Mankato, Minnesota.

CONTENTS

Words in **bold type** are defined on page 24.

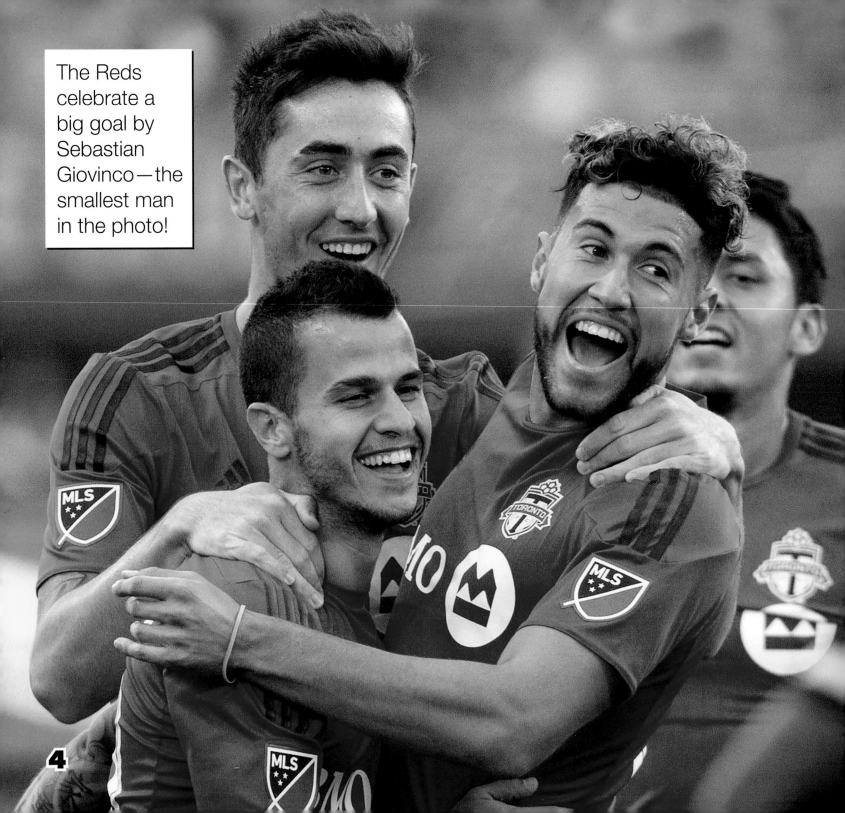

The Reds celebrate a big goal by Sebastian Giovinco—the smallest man in the photo!

MEET TORONTO F.C.

Ice hockey may be Canada's most popular sport, but you would never know it if you were in the stands at a Toronto F.C. game. Toronto F.C. is short for the Toronto Football Club. When people say "football" in most parts of the world they are talking about soccer, not American football.

Toronto fans call their players the Reds. They are among the loudest, proudest sports fans in North America. And on match days, the stadium might be the "reddest" place on the planet!

In 2007, Toronto F.C. played its first season as part of Major League Soccer (MLS). They started very slowly and took many seasons to build a strong club. The fans stayed loyal the whole time. Their loyalty paid off in 2016. The Reds had their first winning record and came within a **penalty kick** of winning the MLS Cup. The team's great stars include Stefan Frei, **Jim Brennan**, Jonathan Osorio, and Dwayne De Rosario.

JIM BRENNAN – DEFENDER

Dwayne De Rosario gives thanks to the fans after scoring a goal against D.C. United in 2009.

Toronto's home field was built to keep soccer fans close to the action.

BEST SEAT IN THE HOUSE

Toronto plays in a stadium built specially for soccer. It holds more than 30,000 fans. It opened in 2007 and is the largest stadium of its kind in Canada. At first the field used artificial turf. The players did not like it, so the city agreed to replace it with grass. In 2016, the field was enlarged so that other sports could be played there.

COLLECTOR'S CORNER

These collectibles show some of the best Toronto players ever.

DWAYNE DE ROSARIO

Midfielder
2009–2011 & 2014
De Rosario was the top midfielder in the league during his time with the Reds. He led the club to three Canadian championships.

JONATHAN OSORIO

Midfielder
First Year with Club: 2013
Osorio was born in Toronto. He became one of the team's best passers.

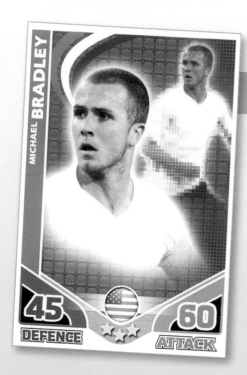

MICHAEL BRADLEY

Midfielder

First Year with Club: 2014

Bradley grew up in a soccer family. His father was coach of the U.S. team in the 2010 **World Cup**.

JOZY ALTIDORE

Striker

First Year with Club: 2015

Toronto fans were happy when Altidore joined the club. He became one of the top scorers in the league.

SEBASTIAN GIOVINCO

Midfielder/Striker

First Year with Club: 2015

Giovinco was a star for many years in Italy before coming to the Reds. He was the best player in MLS in 2015.

WORTHY OPPONENTS

Toronto is one of three MLS teams in Canada. Each year they compete for the Canadian Championship. Other pro teams in Canada also play in the tournament. This makes for a lot of rivalries. Toronto's main rival is the Montreal Impact. They joined MLS in 2012. Fans call it the 401 rivalry because the two cities are connected by Highway 401.

Jozy Altidore battles a Montreal Impact player for a loose ball during a 2015 match.

13

CLUB WAYS

When MLS decided to put a team in Toronto, soccer fans went crazy. They bought 14,000 season tickets. The Reds have many fan clubs. Club members sit in their own special sections. They include the Red Patch Boys, Tribal Rhythm Nation, Kings of the North, and Original 109. Many club members travel to Toronto's away games.

A member of the Red Patch Boys cheers for his team during the 2016 MLS Cup.

ON THE MAP

Toronto brings together players from many countries. These are some of the best:

1. **Tosaint Ricketts** • Edmonton, Alberta, Canada
2. **Drew Moor** • Dallas, Texas
3. **Jozy Altidore** • Livingston, New Jersey
4. **Ryan Johnson** • Kingston, Jamaica
5. **Maicon Santos** • Paracambi, Brazil
6. **Tsubasa Endoh** • Tokyo, Japan
7. **Carl Robinson** • Llandrindod, Wales
8. **Stefan Frei** • Altstatten, Switzerland

NORTH

WEST   EAST

SOUTH

MAP OF NORTH AND CENTRAL AMERICA

Toronto F.C.'s home stadium is in Toronto, Canada.

WORLD MAP

Toronto's crest can be seen on the shoulder of Will Johnson's uniform as he takes a shot against the Red Bulls.

18

KIT AND CREST

Toronto's players wear red from head to toe for their home matches. That is how the team got its nickname. The club's away **kit** is a red and white shirt with blue or red shorts. The team's crest is a shield with the team name and initials. It also has a maple leaf. The maple leaf is a symbol of Canada.

WE WON!

Toronto made it to the MLS Cup in 2016 with one of the most exciting wins in history. The Reds lost their first game against the Montreal Impact, 3–2. In order to make it to the championship game, they had to win the next game by two goals. At the end of 90 minutes, Toronto led 3–2. Each team now had five goals, so they went into extra time. Benoit Cheyrou headed in a goal and Tosaint Ricketts scored another to give Toronto a place in the championship game!

Michael Bradley celebrates with his teammates after they defeated the Montreal Impact in the 2016 playoffs.

FOR THE RECORD

Toronto won the Canadian Championship five times.

Canadian Championship

2009

2010

2011

2012

2016

Benoit Cheyrou was one of the playoff heroes for Toronto in 2016 and also the Most Valuable Player of the Canadian Championship.

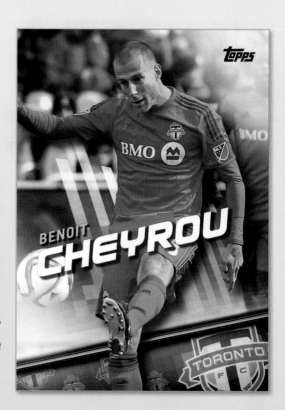

These stars have won major awards while playing for Toronto:

2007	Maurice Edu	• MLS Rookie of the Year
2009	Dwayne De Rosario	• MLS Best XI Midfielder
2009	Dwayne De Rosario	• Canadian Championship MVP
2010	Dwayne De Rosario	• MLS Best XI Midfielder
2010	Dwayne De Rosario	• Canadian Championship MVP
2011	Joao Plata	• Canadian Championship MVP
2011	Dwayne De Rosario	• MLS Best XI Midfielder
2011	Dwayne De Rosario	• MLS Golden Boot
2011	Dwayne De Rosario	• MLS Most Valuable Player
2012	Ryan Johnson	• Canadian Championship MVP
2015	Sebastian Giovinco	• MLS Best XI Forward
2015	Sebastian Giovinco	• MLS Golden Boot
2015	Sebastian Giovinco	• MLS Most Valuable Player
2016	Sebastian Giovinco	• MLS Best XI Forward
2016	Benoit Cheyrou	• Canadian Championship MVP

Soccer Words

Kit
The official league equipment of soccer players, including a club's uniform.

Penalty Kick
A free kick from 12 yards in front of the goal. Only the shooter and goalkeeper are in this play—no defenders are allowed.

World Cup
The championship of soccer. Teams of all nations compete in this tournament every four years.

Index

Photos are on **BOLD** numbered pages.

About the Author

Mark Stewart has been writing about world soccer since the 1990s, including *Soccer: A History of the World's Most Popular Game.* In 2005, he co-authored Major League Soccer's 10-year anniversary book.

About Toronto F.C.

Learn more at these websites:
www.torontofc.ca
www.mlssoccer.com
www.teamspiritextras.com